# INTP

## Utilize Your Strengths, Solve Life's Problems and thrive as the Genius Thinker Type INTP

**The Ultimate Guide To The INTP Personality Type**

Use Your Natural Talents and Personality Traits To Succeed In Your Career, Relationships, and Purpose In Life.

**Dan Johnston**

**Cover Design by Scientist X Designs**

**www.DreamsAroundTheWorld.com**

# CONTENTS

# WHY YOU SHOULD READ THIS BOOK

Do you know those people for whom everything just seems easy?

Their career or business is always getting better. Their relationships appear happy and fulfilling. They have a satisfying home life, work life and, by damn, never seem to have a complaint in the world. **Let's call these people the "Thrivers".**

Then there are those for whom life feels like a constant upward swim. At work, they feel like they don't belong. Their relationships are either problematic or unsatisfying. To them life has always been a struggle. Let's call them the strugglers.

What's going on here? Are some of us just blessed with good fortune? Is everyone else just cursed with constant struggle?

Don't worry; there are no magical forces at work – just some psychology. It's been my experience that there is only one difference between the Strugglers and the Thrivers.

The Thrivers, by reflection, study, or just dumb luck, have built their lives around their natural personalities. Their work utilizes their strengths while their relationships complement their weaknesses.

A small percentage of the Thrivers came into their lives "naturally". The careers their parents or teachers recommended were the perfect fit for them, or they had a gut feeling that turned out to be right. They met their ideal partner who complemented them perfectly. I believe, however, that this group is the minority.

Most Thrivers have spent years "watching" themselves and reflecting about who they really are. For some this is a natural process, for others (myself included) it's a more deliberate process. We read, studied, questioned and took tests all in the name of self-awareness. We've made it a priority to know and understand ourselves.

Whatever a Thriver learns about themselves, they use to make significant changes in their life. They change careers, end relationships and start new hobbies. They do all this so that one day their life will be fulfilling and have a natural flow to it: a life in which they can thrive.

This book is for Thrivers: Past, present and future.

If you once had your flow but can't seem to find it again, read on.

If you're in your flow and want to keep and improve it, read on.

And if you're one of the beautiful souls struggling but committed to finding your flow and thriving, you're in the right place. Read on.

Today you may feel like a salmon swimming upstream, but this is a temporary state of being. One day soon, you will find yourself evolving. Perhaps into a dolphin, swimming amongst those with whom you belong, free to be yourself, to play and to enjoy life. Maybe you'd rather find your place as a whale - wise and powerful, roaming the oceans and setting your own path, respected and admired by all.

*KNOWLEDGE BRINGS AWARENESS AND
AWARENESS BRINGS SUCCESS*

I'm an entrepreneur as well as a writer. As an entrepreneur, negotiation plays a big part in any success I might have. One of the secrets to being a good negotiator is to always be the one with the most information in the room. The same holds true for decision making in our personal lives.

When it comes to the big things in life, we can't make a good decision if we don't have all the relevant information.

I think most of us understand this on an external level. When we're shopping for a new car, we research our options: the prices, the engines, and the warranties. We find out as much as we can to help make our decision.

Unfortunately, we often forget the most important factor in our decisions: Us.

A Ford Focus is a better economic decision and a more enjoyable drive than a SUV...but that doesn't matter if you're 7 feet tall or have 5 kids who need to be driven to Hockey in the snow.

When it comes to life decisions, such as our work or relationships, who we are is the most important decision factor.

It doesn't matter if all your friends say he is the perfect guy...it only matters if he's perfect for you. It doesn't matter if your family wants you to be a lawyer, a doctor or an accountant...what do you want to do? If you make your decision based on what the outside world says, you won't find the levels of happiness or fulfillment you desire.

In order to make the best decisions for you, you must first know yourself. That is the purpose of this book: To provide the most in-depth information on the INTP personality type available anywhere.

## By Reading This Book You Will:

- Improve self-awareness.
- Uncover your natural strengths.
- Understand your weaknesses.
- Discover new career opportunities.
- Learn how to have better relationships.
- Develop a greater understanding of your family, partner and friends.
- Have the knowledge to build your ideal life around your natural personality.
- Have more happiness, health, love, money and all round life success while feeling more focused and fulfilled.

# FREE READER-ONLY EXCLUSIVES: WORKBOOK AND BONUSES

When I wrote this book, I set out to create the most *useful* guide available. I know there will always be bigger or more detailed textbooks out there, but how many of them are actually helpful?

To help you get the most from this book I have created a collection of free extras to support you along the way. To download these, simply visit the special section of my website: www.dreamsaroundtheworld.com/thrive

You will be asked to enter your email address so I can send you the "Thriving Bonus Pack". You'll receive:

- A 5-part mini-course (delivered via email) with tips on how to optimize your life so you can maximize your strengths and thrive.
- A compatibility chart showing how you are most likely to relate to the other 15 personality types. You'll discover which people are likely to become good friends (or more) and who you should avoid at all costs.
- A PDF workbook to ramp up the results you'll get from this book. It's formatted to be printed, so you can fill in your answers to the exercises in each chapter as you go.

To download the Thriving Bonus Pack visit:

www.DreamsAroundTheWorld.com/thrive

# INTRODUCTION TO THIS SERIES

The goal of this series is to provide a clear window into the strengths, weaknesses, opportunities and challenges of each type.

I want you to have every advantage possible in the areas of work, play, relationships, health and finance.

You'll discover new things about yourself and find new ways to tap into your strengths and create a life where you thrive.

This book is part of a series; each one focuses on one type. You will find I write directly to you, although I do not make an assumption as to your personality type or your traits. I will generally refer to the type, aka INTP, instead of saying "you". Not every trait of a type applies to everyone of that type, and we never want to make any assumptions about who you are or your limitations.

I would recommend beginning with your type to learn most about yourself, but don't stop there. Each book focuses on a particular type and will be valuable for that type, as well as family, friends, bosses and colleagues of that type.

Even before writing these books I found myself doing extensive reading on the types of my brother, parents, friends and even dates. In my business I would research the types of my assistants, employees and potential business partners. I found that learning about myself got me 60% of the way, and the other 40% came from learning about the other people in my life.

If you plan to read up on all the different types I suggest looking at my "Collection" books, which include multiple types all in one book for a reduced price. It'll be easier and a better price for you than buying each individual book.

# DISCLAIMER

I know this book will serve you in discovering your strengths and building your self-awareness. I have researched and written this book based on years of practical experience including running multiple businesses, talking to dozens of people about their strengths and weaknesses, and applying this knowledge to my own life to discover my strengths and build a business around what I do best. With that said, I must emphasize that I am not a psychologist, psychiatrist or counselor, or in any way qualified to offer medical advice. The information in this book is intended to improve your life but it does not replace professional advice in any way and is not legal, medical or psychiatric advice. So, if you're in a bad place or may be suffering from a mental illness please seek professional help!

# DISCOVERING THE "ARCHITECT": WHO IS AN INTP?

On the surface, INTPs are reserved and analytical, often lost in their thoughts or an attempt at solving their latest theoretical problem. While not social butterflies, when they choose to be, many INTPs are charming, witty, and well regarded by their peers.

INTPs aren't interested in social customs they see as illogical or as barriers to the pursuit of knowledge. Along this same thread, they distrust authority and job titles, and see these as obstacles standing in the way of new ideas. Instead, the INTP believes an idea should be judged by its merit, regardless of the seniority, status, or esteem of the individual behind it.

INTPs value autonomy and autonomous minded people. INTPs aren't as comfortable in social situations but do enjoy the company of those with similar interests. They also enjoy long periods of time on their own, pondering problems and coming up with solutions. Given this way of being, INTPs usually prefer to work alone versus in groups (whether as a leader or follower).

INTPs are drawn to theories, and their understanding of a topic is based on their ability to understand and articulate the main principles. Once they articulate for themselves, they have a brilliant ability to explain complex concepts and ideas to others in easy to understand terms. This ability extends itself, and in fact thrives, in the written context. INTPs feel a need to understand an idea or discussion from all the applicable angles. When debating, INTPs are extremely impatient when facing weak or indefensible ideas, and will go on the attach with devastating consequences for their adversary.

In other times, the INTPs' intelligence and ability to grasp complex ideas can leave their explanations filled with unnecessary details, leaving listeners confused. At this point listeners, or readers, may think the INTP is intentionally making things harder than necessary. In reality, the INTP is just attempting to crystalize the concept by presenting as much relevant material as possible.

It should come as no surprise that INTPs frequently prosper in careers related to science, architecture, law, psychology and philosophy. Within these fields their ability to examine and explain complex ideas from all points of view is particularly valuable.

# INTRODUCTION TO MYERS BRIGGS

I first discovered Myers Briggs about 5 years ago, although I do have some vague memories of taking a career test in High School. I'm sure that test was likely Myers-Briggs, but who really pays attention to those when you're 16?

Myers-Briggs is one of many options in the world of personality profiles and testing. It is arguably the most popular, and in my opinion it is the best place to start because the results provide insight into all aspects of our lives whereas other tests are often very focused on just career.

Myers-Briggs is based on the idea that we are all different. These differences aren't simply a result of conditioning (as some behavioral psychologists used to argue) but rather a difference in how we're wired.

This doesn't mean that we can't build certain traits, or that any traits are 100% natural. Rather, Myers-Briggs is an opportunity to learn which traits come most naturally to you and which areas you may find challenging or need to invest time in developing.

It's also an opportunity to understand the people around us and get to the root of many conflicts. In fact, understanding the different types and how they relate to others could be the most valuable aspect of Myers-Briggs for many people.

# THE 16 TYPES AND FOUR GROUPS

Myers-Briggs includes 16 different personality types that are described by a unique series of 4 letters.

At first, the types appear confusing, but they're really quite simple.

Each type is based on one of two modes of being or thinking for each of the four letters.

- E (extrovert) or I (introvert)
- N (intuitive) or S (sensing)
- T (thinking) or F (feeling)
- P (perceiving) or J (judging)

Now, don't pay too much attention to the words tied to each letter because they don't actually offer a great description for the characteristic.

In just a second I'll share my explanation for each letter. Just before this, I want to share an important point to remember: Personality analysis and profiling is a bit of an art, as well as a science. In other words, since people are so diverse, the descriptions and results aren't always black and white. Some people have a strong preference for one mode or the other, but others are closer to the middle. It's natural for all of us to occasionally feel or demonstrate traits of the other types.

What we want to focus on here is your natural way of being and the functions you are strongest in. It is also important to know that you can, and will, develop your secondary (or auxiliary) and third (or tertiary) "functions" over time and with practice. In doing so, you will create a more balanced personality, with less weak spots, and a more diverse set of skills. In fact, the key to overcoming most personality challenges is to develop your weaker functions.

Generally it's said that we grow our primary function in our early years, our secondary in our twenties and thirties, and our third function some time in our thirties and forties. However, this assumes you're not being proactive and reading a book like this one. In your case, there is no reason you can't leap ahead a few decades and strengthen your other functions ahead of schedule.

## WHAT THE FOUR LETTERS MEAN

As you know, there are 4 letters that make up your personality type.

At first these letters can be a little confusing, especially since their descriptions aren't the most telling.

Here's how I explain each letter.

**For the first letter in your type, you are either an E, or an I.**

The E or I describe how we relate with other people and social situations.

Extroverts are drawn to people, groups, and new social situations. They are generally comfortable at parties and in large groups.

Introverts are more reserved. This is not to say Introverts do now enjoy people, they do. Introverts are just happier in smaller groups, and with people they know and trust like friends or family. Keep in mind, this does not mean that Introverts are not capable of mastering social skills if they must. Rather, they will not be drawn to such situations or find the process as exciting or enjoyable as an extrovert would.

"The Deal Breaker": For some people E or I is obvious. For others the line is blurred. This question will make your preference clear: "Does being around new people or groups add to or drain your energy? If you spent an entire day alone would you feel "off" or bad, or would you be just fine?" If you can spend a day or two alone without feeling bad, or if spending a few hours in a group of people leaves you feeling tired, you're an Introvert.

While Extroverts may often steal a lot of the attention in a room, Introverts often have the upper hand. While many Extroverts crave the spotlight, Introverts are able to sit back and calmly observe, learning more about a situation and making their contributions more meaningful and impactful.

Further, Introverts have the ability to work alone for long periods. In many professions, such as writing, this is a significant advantage.

INTPs are Introverts. This is why INTPs are so capable at working alone, are self-sufficient, and usually not interested in building large social groups.

## For the second letter, you are either an N or an S.

This trait describes how we interact with the world.

Those with the intuitive trait (N) tend to be introspective and imaginative. They enjoy theoretical discussions and "big picture" kind of ideas. For an extreme example, imagine a philosophy professor with a stained suit jacket and a terribly messy office.

Of course, this isn't the reality for most Ns. Most intuitive people live a happy, fulfilled life full of new ideas and inspirations…all while managing the day-to-day aspects of their lives at an acceptable level. Ns have an exceptional imagination and ability to form new ideas, tell stories, and inspire those around them.

Those with the Sensor trait are observant and in touch with their immediate environment. They prefer practical, "hands on" information to theory. They prefer facts over ideas. For an extreme example, think of a mechanic or military strategist.

INTPs have the intuitive trait. This is why they are drawn to ideas and have a great imagination and ability to problem solve.

## Third, you are either a T or an F.

This trait describes how you make decisions and come to conclusions, as well as what role emotions play in our personalities and how we deal with them.

Those with the thinker trait are "tough-minded". They tend to be objective and impersonal with others. This can make them appear uncaring, but they are generally very fair. Those with the thinking trait rely on logic and rational arguments for their decisions. The "T" trait would be common amongst (successful) investors and those who need to make impersonal and objective decisions in their careers.

Those with the feeler trait are personal, friendly and sympathetic with others. Their decisions are often influenced by their emotions or the "people" part of a situation. They are also more sensitive and impacted by their emotions, and less afraid to show their emotions to the outside world. The "F" trait would be common amongst counselors and psychologists.

INTPs have the thinker trait. This is why INTPs can be so logical. It is also why INTPs may have trouble empathizing or connecting with more emotional people.

## Lastly, you are either a P or a J.

This trait describes how we organize information in our internal and external worlds. This translates into how we schedule ourselves, stay organized, and evaluate our options.

Perceivers are best described as "Probers" or "Explorers". They look for options, opportunities and alternatives; this means they tend to be more creative, open minded and, well, often have messy bedrooms. They're happy to give one plan a try without all the details, knowing they can adjust or try something else in the future.

Judgers are structured and organized. They tend to be more consistent and scheduled. Spreadsheets may be their friends and their rooms will be clean...or at least organized. They prefer concrete plans and closure over openness and possibilities.

You would find more Ps amongst artists and creative groups, whereas professions like accountants and engineers would be almost exclusively Js.

INTPs have the Perceiving trait. This feeds their creativity and adaptability. It is why they have great imaginations, are able to come up with new ideas, and are happy proceeding with a plan before all the details are worked out.

## THE FOUR GROUPS

Since the original creation of the 16 types, Psychologists have recognized 4 distinct groups, each containing 4 types. The 4 types within each group have distinct traits in common based on sharing 2 of the 4 traits.

The 4 types are:

- The Artisans (The SPs)
- The Guardians (The SJs)
- The Idealists (The NFs)
- The Rationals (The NTs)

As an INTP you are a Rational.

Rationals greatest strength is strategy. They are intellectual in speech, and utilitarian in how they pursue their goals.

They are seekers of knowledge and trust reason and logic over emotions and feelings. They seek to gain as much information as possible and apply this knowledge towards long term plans for achieving their goals.

Not known for their empathy, Rationals are considered tough minded in how they deal with others. The truth is, Rationals strive to be honest and fair in their decision making and how they treat people. So even though they may come off as cold or uncaring, their actual decisions are usually very fair and objective.

The other 3 Rational types, your cousins, are:

- The Fieldmarshals and Executives: ENTJs

- The Charming Visionary: ENTPs

- The Strategic Mastermind: INTJs

To learn more about how all the types relate and interact, download the free compatibility chart at:

www.DreamsAroundTheWorld.com/thrive

# ADVICE FROM INTPS FOR INTPS

After publishing the first edition of this book I reached out to a group of INTPs. I asked them what advice they would share with a younger, perhaps less experienced, INTP that would help them live the best life possible.

I thought I would include a few of their answers in this updated edition, and what better place than here.

So, allow me to present their telling, and mostly unedited, answers:

"Try enjoying things the more extroverted types do naturally, but within your comfort zone, or at its edge. The more you do so, the more you'll expand your comfort zone and as an analysing perceptive type, you'll quickly pick up on loosening up in these situations.

For me, I went to the pub one hell of a lot. I drank like crazy, smoked like a house on fire and generally enjoyed myself with huge confidence post realising who most people are. These days it's a breeze, fun even.

I suppose it's about unlocking yourself, and for me... Well, liquor was the key that set the monkey free."

"Don't let the label of INTP turn you into a whining victim. Take control of your own life."

"Being young equals stupidity. You're going to be and there's really no changing it. Once you have about 30 years under your belt, experience starts to kick in and you start to metamorphis into an adult and realize your parents weren't as stupid as you thought. The one good thing about being young is you tend to act before thinking and usually accomplish more during that time than you ever will later in life."

"In the depth of your solitude you find joy, yet you yearn for company, and try to break the shelters of ice between you and other individuals, but once you mingle again with them, you change your mind, you discover that ice is deep within you, that's why even in the coldest weather you don't feel anything. It's a constant cycle, but in time you learn, and everyday you grow wiser, and your functions develop better, you control them more, and in the end you die, perhaps even a horrific death, who knows? (possibly even flattened to a nearly two-dimensional layer by a tar-flattening vehicle, or worse)"

"Say yes, you've already said no too many times.

Congrats. Now try not to second guess yourself (that's already someone else's job).

You're smart and those around you probably know it. There isn't always a need to give a complete explanation. Keep it simple and learn when to stop.

"Go out of your way to be different from your surroundings, even if it means conforming to the thing others are trying to escape. But don't do it just so others can see your individuality. This is a something for you to enjoy alone. There's nothing more satisfying than passive, introspective rebellion from social consensus."


This section of the book will always be growing. If you're an "experienced" INTP and you'd like to add your insight, wisdom and advice to upcoming editions, you can email me at: me@thedanjohnston.com.

# IN GOOD COMPANY: FAMOUS INTPS

As an INTP, you are amongst some very good company. In this chapter you'll find a collection of famous and "successful" people who are either confirmed, or suspected, as being INTPs.

Do not use this chapter as a guide to what you must do or who you must be like. Rather, use this chapter as a source of inspiration. It is a chance to see what's possible as an INTP and what great things have been accomplished by those who share a similar makeup to you.

Personally, I have found great value in studying famous people from my own type including reading their autobiographies. Most of us spend the early years of our lives feeling lost and trying to figure out our purpose or how we want to end up. I've found studying those of my type who have found their purpose, and then success, gives me a shortcut to understanding my own potential and the directions my life could go.

## FAMOUS INTPS

**Scientists, Writers and Thought Leaders**
- Hannah Arendt
- Albert Einstein
- Richard Dawkins
- Charles Darwin
- Immanuel Kant
- John Locke
- Parmenides
- Adam Smith
- Marie Curie
- James Madison
- Rene Descartes

**Actors and Performers**
- Sigourney Weaver
- Charlotte Gainsbourg
- Jesse Eisenberg
- David Cronenberg
- Tina Fey
- Ben Stein

- Thucydides

**Politicians and Leaders**
Newt Gingrich
Barack Obama (According to some)
Benjamin Franklin (Inventor and politician)
Henry Kissinger

*Worth Noting:* If you haven't yet read on any of the other types you may not notice the distinctions of the famous INTPs. Compared with other types, famous INTPs tend to find success with their minds. They are famous for coming up with original and brilliant ideas that change how people think (Einstein, Darwin).

In business and their career, they find the most success when they avoid politics and bureaucratic organizations and instead go out on their own and create something original.

## GOING DEEPER EXERCISE

Of the famous INTPs on this list, which are you most familiar with?

What are some common elements you notice? These could be specific personality traits or characteristics. It could also include actions they have taken or tough decisions they have made. For example: Going against the grain or choosing to follow a passion.

# YOUR SECRET WEAPONS

(Aka your unique strengths)

In my own life I have found no greater success secret than discovering, *and applying*, my strengths.

When we are young we're often taught that we need to be good at many things. For example, schools are based on your average grade and most parents would prefer their child have a smooth report card of all B+s than one with two A+s and two C-s.

The real world doesn't reward the well-rounded individual, at least not exceptionally well. Those who receive the greatest rewards are those who focus on their strengths and ignore all else. Think of people like Arnold Schwarzenegger, Steve Jobs and Oprah Winfrey.

Does anyone *really* care if Oprah is bad at math, if Arnold has trouble managing his personal life or if Steve Jobs was a bit of an ass to employees from time to time?

Nope. No one cares because each of these Greats focused on their strengths and created an extraordinary life for themselves.

Oprah (an ENFJ) harnessed her empathy and ability to build trust and bond with people to create incredible interviews and connect with her audience.

Arnold (an INTJ) used his focus, discipline, and strategic thinking to achieve incredible goals in fitness, performing and politics despite being the underdog in almost everything he ever did.

Steve Jobs (an I.S.T.P.) kept his energy focused on his creative and visual strengths. His vision was so clear, and his innovations so impressive, that his social graces didn't matter.

Now, as you read on you will discover the unique strengths closely linked to INTPs. While you read this remember that these are the strengths that come naturally to you, but you still need to develop and fine-tune them if you want to thrive.

## AN INTP's SECRET WEAPONS

- Thinking big and creating new ideas.
- Thinking big and creating new ideas. Seriously though, I can't emphasize this enough. INTPs have a special ability to go into their zone and deeply focus on an idea or problem. This, combined with their usually high intelligence and love of original thought, often leads to the INTP being the leading thinker or guru in their area of expertise.
- INTPs can be somewhat charming and are usually well liked. They are good-natured and often have a nice sense of humour. Like other "idea" types, they are also fairly laid back and low maintenance, rarely involving themselves in personal drama.
- INTPs have exceptionally precise communication skills. Perhaps not the most charismatic, their strength is in accurately and completely communicating an idea so it can be properly understood by others in their field.
- INTPs are "chill". It's easy to get along with them and they go with the flow, rarely causing problems or disagreements.
- Overall, INTPs are bright and intelligent.
- INTPs are very adaptive and can function well in most situations. They're comfortable with change.
- Thinking of new ways to do things others have missed.
- INTPs' quickness is tied to their perceptiveness and intelligence. As part of these same abilities, they're able to see connections between situations and ideas that most others miss. This often leads them to create new ideas.

## Highly Developed INTPs Will Enjoy Even More Super Powers:

- Being genius (literally) problem solvers and inventors. Many intellectual breakthroughs, from sciences and technology to philosophy and economics, have come from the mind of an INTP.
- An understanding, and following, of values. Despite being logical thinkers they are able to see the long term benefits of having personal values and principles.
- A desire to create close personal relationships, and knowing how to support, nurture and grow them.

## In summary, a developed INTP can be:

- Insightful
- Ingenious
- Creative
- Intelligent
- Logical
- Quick
- Adaptable
- Creative
- Well Liked
- Supportive
- Inspiring
- Innovative

## Keys To Using Your Strengths as an INTP

1. Make time to spend with people and allow your mind to relax…often it is during this "down time" when the best ideas are formulated.

2.  Avoid being the "finisher" on projects and surround yourself with people who value your ideas and are willing to put in the "grunt work" to support you and your ideas.

3.  It's easy to get trapped in your head or your ideas. Start a hobby or activity that involves something physical, such as a sport, outdoor activity or artistic craft. This will help you get out of your head and connect your ideas with the world around you.

In this and future chapters, you will discover "Going Deeper" exercises. These are designed to help you better understand and apply the chapter's content. If you're like me you may want to write your answers down. When you bought this book you also got access to a companion workbook you can print and then fill in with your answers as you go. You can download the workbook for free at:

www.DreamsAroundTheWorld.com/thrive

# GOING DEEPER EXERCISE

Of the strengths listed above, which most jump out at you as strengths of your own?

_______________________________________________

_______________________________________________

_______________________________________________

_______________________________________________

_______________________________________________

What are 3 strengths listed above that you know you have but are not actively using in your life, at least not as much as you know you should?

_______________________________________________

_______________________________________________

_______________________________________________

_______________________________________________

_______________________________________________

How could you apply these strengths more frequently?

_______________________________________________

_______________________________________________

_______________________________________________

_______________________________________________

_______________________________________________

# YOUR KRYPTONITE

(Aka your potential weaknesses)

You didn't think I was going to stop at your strengths did you? As much as I say *focus on your strengths* it is still important to be aware of your weaknesses, even if it is just so you can more easily ignore them.

Below you will find a list of weaknesses, or challenges, common amongst INTPs. As with strengths, this is not a definitive list and do not take it as a prescription for how INTPs have to be.

Sometimes I will see posts in a Facebook group for a specific type where people seem overly proud of their type challenges. I remember one post on an ENFP group making light at how the poster had been unable to tidy their room in 4 days. While it was good for a "we've all been there" chuckle, I did find myself turned off at what a chaotic life this person must have. They have chosen to neither fix their weakness (by developing their self-discipline and follow through) nor embrace it (by hiring a maid). Instead, they have chosen to suffer what they described as 4 days of agony simply trying to clean a room.

So if some of these weaknesses don't really resonate with you, **good**. Ignore them and don't assume you should be weak in that area if you're not. If you do connect with some of the weaknesses, take it as an opportunity to either work to improve that area of yourself, or to accept the weakness and find a solution so you don't have to deal with it.

Many of the INTPs' challenges tend to revolve around their underdeveloped extroverted intuition function and an overdeveloped introverted thinking. This leads to their other functions, such as how they interact with the world (extroverted intuition), being used to serve their internal thoughts and judgements. This means perceiving everything with confirmation bias, trying to justify or "back up" what they already know instead of objectively looking for new information. This can all lead to an INTP's thoughts getting out of control, coming to conclusions that aren't objective or based on the real world, and then ultimately isolating themselves.

As you read these, remember they are only a result of an underdeveloped personality and can easily be overcome by developing weaker areas.

## COMMON KRYPTONITE FOR THE INTP

While studying INTP's potential Kryptonite, I noticed a few patterns and root causes. I've decided to group some of the Kryptonite behaviors under their root causes here...although they are all somewhat related and intertwined.

Until they develop their full personality so it serves them beyond their introverted intuition, most INTPs will have experienced some level of challenge in some of the following areas to one degree or another.

**Before they fully develop their personalities, some INTPs may:**

- Be somewhat clueless about how to dress or conduct themselves in social situations. This lack of social graces may contribute to some of the fears discussed in the next points.
- Unleash extreme emotions under stress; far more than the situation calls for.
- Have trouble expressing their inner thoughts and feelings with other people.

**Fear of Being Rejected or Looking Stupid**

- A fear of being rejected, being wrong, or looking stupid all leads to a deep fear of being vulnerable. Ultimately, if one puts themselves out there in a new social situation or with a new idea there is always a risk of rejection. Successful INTPs know this and are courageous enough to take risks and put themselves out there (and in the process sharing their genius with the world).

- Can fall into a "comfort rut" where they avoid anything new or uncomfortable. During this time they will often reinforce their own (often negative) beliefs about society or other people. It's important they break this rut as soon as possible and focus on experimenting the world as it is.

- Rejecting people who think or act differently than themselves, often rejecting or insulting the people themselves in the process and being unaware of the hurt they cause. This behavior may be a defense mechanism but it does not serve the INTP and can lead to social isolation.

## Need To Be Right (and to feel significant or special)

- Rejecting new ideas that don't fit into their world view or support their own experience of the world.

- In some cases, they can develop rather paranoid theories about people trying to control them. This behavior has the possibility to gain unfavorable momentum if the INTP continues to reject ideas or evidence which is different from their own beliefs.

## OVERCOMING YOUR WEAKNESSES

Many of the INTP's weaknesses share a single root cause. If they do not develop their secondary function, extroverted intuition, INTPs' other functions can become slave to their introverted thinking and skew or distort everything they experience in order to serve the beliefs of their introverted thinking (and proving they are "right").

Taken as individual characteristics, this list of potential weaknesses only offers a description, not hope for change. Yet, if you take time to really read and re-read you will start to notice patterns, understand root causes, and perhaps see what can be a vicious cycle.

For example, an INTP may have trouble expressing themselves as well as handling social etiquette. This could lead to some early childhood rejections or embarrassing situations (we've all been there!). These events could traumatize the INTP and be the beginning of their need to be right and desire to avoid uncomfortable situations. Of course, when we begin to avoid uncomfortable social situations our social abilities begin to deteriorate and a vicious cycle begins.

## GOING DEEPER EXERCISE

Of the weaknesses listed above, which 3 do you most recognize in yourself?

_______________________________________________

_______________________________________________

_______________________________________________

_______________________________________________

What are 3 weaknesses listed above that you know are having a significant negative impact on your success?

_______________________________________________

_______________________________________________

_______________________________________________

_______________________________________________

_______________________________________________

How could you reduce the impact these weaknesses have on your life, either by learning to overcome them or eliminating the activities that bring them to the surface?

_______________________________________________

_______________________________________________

_______________________________________________

_______________________________________________

_______________________________________________

# IDEAL CAREER OPTIONS FOR AN INTP

If you gave a Myers-Briggs test to a group of a few hundred people from the same profession you would see a very clear pattern.

An Accountant in my martial arts class told me that of 600 Chartered Accountants who took the Myers-Briggs test at his firm, he was one of only 3 people who didn't score the same type.

This happens for two reasons:

1) Selection Bias: People with the personality type for accounting will tend to do well in related tasks and receive hints that that kind of work is right for them. They may especially enjoy numbers, spreadsheets etc.
2) Survival Bias: Those with the personality type for accounting are most likely to pass the vigorous tests and internships required to become a Charted Accountant.

We are actually much better at finding the right path for us than we give ourselves credit for. In almost every profession, there is a significantly higher percentage of those "typed" to excel in it than random chance would have.

Yet, many people still slip through the cracks, or spend decades searching for that perfect career before finding it.

This chapter will help you avoid the cracks and stop wasting your precious time. Below, you'll find a comprehensive list of careers INTPs tend to be drawn to and succeed in.

There are many more career options beyond this list that I have seen in other books and intentionally not included here.

These include "good" options that an INTP could easily do and succeed in, but would not be as happy or fulfilled as they would in another profession where they could use their real strengths.

I have included only the options I believe INTPs have an upper hand in *and* the highest likelihood to find fulfillment and success. There are always other options, but why swim upstream if you don't need to, right?

**To be most successful, an INTP should focus on work that:**

- Allows for creative contribution, problem solving, and new approaches and ideas.
- Allows the INTP to explore new ideas and approaches including theoretical, creative and processes.
- Is performed within a flexible structure and a laid back environment and gives them enough time, freedom and autonomy to operate spontaneously without excessive rules or limitations.
- Gives them enough time and flexibility to process ideas at their own pace and follow hunches or inspirations.
- Acknowledges and rewards original thought, proficiency and the ability to improvise with credit going to the INTP for their contributions.
- Allows them to be the "Starter" on projects and does not force them to handle the details of the ideas they come up with.
- Allows the INTP to spend time with a small group of highly regarded people they admire and respect.
- Includes spending time around powerful individuals they aspire to be like and have the opportunity to grow themselves and their own power.

## POPULAR PROFESSIONS FOR INTPS

**Creative**

- Photographer
- Creative writer
- Artist
- Entertainer/dancer
- Musician
- Inventor
- Informational-graphics designer
- Music arranger and orchestrator
- Director
- Film editor
- Art director

**In The Business World**

- Investigator
- Intellectual property attorney
- Legal mediator
- Corporate finance attorney
- Entrepreneur
- Venture capitalist
- Investment banker
- Business analyst
- Lawyer
- Member of think-tank/research team
- Economist
- New product creator (ideas)
- Financial analyst
- Architect
- Entertainment agent
- Intelligence specialist

**Technology and Computers**

- Computer software designer
- Computer programmer
- Research and development specialist
- Network integration specialist
- Programmer
- Network administrator
- Internet architect
- Web developer
- Computer animator
- Computer engineer

**Academic and Sciences**

- Mathematician
- Archaeologist
- Philosopher
- Researcher
- Biomedical Engineer
- Microbiologist
- Geneticist
- Economist
- Astronomer
- Neurologist
- Physicist
- Plastic surgeon
- Pharmacist

- Java programmer/analyst
- Software developer
- Scientist
- Physicist
- Biophysicist
- Anthropologist
- Pharmaceutical researcher

## GOING DEEPER EXERCISE

Read through the list above and answer the following questions.

1)  Which 5-10 careers jump out at you as something you'd enjoy doing?

________________________________

________________________________

________________________________

________________________________

________________________________

2)  Thinking back to the sections on strengths, what do you notice about the list of careers? What strengths might contribute to success in these careers?

________________________________

________________________________

________________________________

________________________________

________________________________

# THRIVING AT WORK

There is an astronomical difference between a job you're good at and a career you love and in which you thrive.

While some people are fine just getting by, people like you and I sure aren't. This section will help you thrive at work.

## 3 Foundations For Thriving At Work

1) Be aware of your strengths and weaknesses and be selective of the work you do. Be honest in job interviews about where you excel as well as where you struggle.

2) When in a job, take this same honest approach with your supervisor. Explain that you aren't being lazy; rather you feel you could deliver much more *value* to the company by focusing on your strengths.

3) At least once per week, if not daily, stop for a few minutes and ask yourself if you're working in your strengths or struggling in your weaknesses. Remember, you have unique and valuable gifts…but only if you make the effort to use them and avoid getting trapped in the wrong kind of work.

## Secret Weapons At Work

When it comes to your work, be sure to tap into these work related strengths for INTPs:

- Ability to see the big picture and understand the consequences of certain actions or ideas.
- The ability to think outside the box and find new possibilities.
- Adaptability. Can quickly change directions.
- Rational and methodical thinking. A developed INTP will be able to think through a situation and come to the right

conclusion about what action to take (even when they're under stress).

- Impartial thinking: INTPs are able to take on work that isn't aligned with their values without guilt or reservations. For instance, an INTP lawyer would have no issues with defending a criminal she knew to be guilty.
- INTPs can be objective and think through an issue without taking it personally or letting their own values bias their decision.
- Ability to see the big picture and understand the consequences of certain actions or ideas.
- Independent. Able to jump into a project, take risks, and just do it without much supervision or guidance. This includes having confidence in their ideas and the courage to move forward with them.
- Being quick to merge information and put multiple ideas together.
- INTPs have an all-round love of knowledge and intellectual curiosity. This means they have very well developed research abilities and a strong drive to expand their knowledge in whatever area they take on.
- Courage to try new things, take risks, and find ways to overcome the obstacles that inevitably come along with something new.

# KRYPTONITE AT WORK

To maximize their success, INTPs should be aware of some challenges they face at work. INTPs will not always, but **may:**

- Be impatient with people or organizations they see as incompetent or ineffective. This can play out as the employee feeling smarter than their boss and angry their intelligence and contributions aren't properly rewarded.
- Be impatient with people or organizations they see as inflexible or unimaginative.
- Be disorganized or unscheduled.
- Have trouble prioritizing tasks or planning their work and therefore can be indecisive as to what to do next.
- Can become so theoretical in their thinking that they forget reality; the ideas that come from this thinking then have little or no practical value.
- Promise more than they can actually deliver on or misrepresent their abilities. This isn't intentional; it's just a result of their optimism and enthusiasm.
- Be impatient with those who are less creative than them, or those who tend to "ponder" things before making a decision.
- Struggle simplifying complex ideas so they can be (quickly) explained to others.
- Lack the discipline to complete tasks or follow through on details.
- Dislike ridged or routine tasks, people or systems.
- -Easily become bored or sidetracked when the exciting part of a project ends or when confronted by repetitive tasks.

# RICH AND HAPPY RELATIONSHIPS

Whoever said opposites attract never met an ENFP + ISTJ couple.

Sure, you want a partner who complements your strengths and weaknesses, but most of us also want someone who understands us: someone with whom we can express our opinions and ideas and be understood.

In this section we'll start with a discussion on what INTPs are like in relationships. Then we'll look at the most common personality types INTPs are happy with. Lastly, we will end with some advice on creating and maintaining successful relationships as an INTP, and *with* an INTP.

## INTPs in Relationships

INTPs are faithful and devoted mates and take their relationships seriously. Often preoccupied with their ideas, INTPs can be aloof partners, forgetting appointments, birthdays and anniversaries.

If left up to them, INTPs will spent their time in books and ideas and give little time to their physical needs or relationship maintenance. It's best for the relationship that their partner takes charge of planning their time together and social events.

## INTPs' Ideal Matches

A note on compatibility: There is no be all and end all. The information on type compatibility is either based on theory or surveys, neither of which will ever provide a universal rule.

NT (rational) types find the greatest relationship *satisfaction* dating NFs. This is likely because they can share a common way of thinking about the world. With that said, a few of the most compatible matches for INTPs are ENFJs, ENTJs and ESTJs.

Ultimately, the two individuals involved, and their desire to grow and work to create an incredible relationship, will have the biggest determination of their success together. The one incompatibility that I've noticed time and time again is between Intuitives (Ns) and Sensors (Ss). I think this is because these two groups have fundamentally different ways of interacting with the world and often have trouble understanding one another.

In my own experience in romantic relationships, friendships, and business partnerships, I (a strong Intuitive – ENFP), have always run into trouble with those who rate highly on the Sensor mode of being.

Beyond that, it's all up in the air. Generally, for organization sake, I would suggest that Ps match with a J. The P will benefit from the J's structure and organization, and the J will benefit from the P's creativity and spontaneity.

## TIPS FOR DATING AS AN INTP

1. INTPs don't enjoy life's details. Cleaning, organization, scheduling…it's not nearly as appealing as the next big idea. Consider a partner with strengths in these areas to complement you.

2. You're likely pretty low maintenance and you value focused time with your ideas and projects. To avoid conflict you need a confident partner who will give you both emotional and time freedom to do your own thing.

3. You may have trouble hitting the eject button on a bad relationship. If your relationship isn't meeting your needs, speak to someone you trust for an objective opinion. Your loyalty, caring and desire to make things work could be blinding you to reality.

4.  INTPs don't always know the right thing to say, especially in more intimate or vulnerable moments. Sometimes they do know what to say but just don't understand the value of expressing it so they hold back. Whatever the reasons for "holding back", your partner will be much happier if you learn to express yourself and try and say what they need to hear to be happy.

5.  If they feel forced into a commitment or closeness they aren't ready for or comfortable with, an INTP won't hesitate to run. Be aware of this impulse in yourself and try to objectively think it through. If a relationship is getting too close too fast, take a moment and express your discomfort to your partner before it's too late. If it's already "too late", ask yourself what is really so bad and why you feel this desire to flee?

# Tips For Dating An INTP

(If you're an INTP, and you agree with the ideas in this next section, you may want to share it with your partner).

1. INTPs have trouble expressing their feelings. Try and help them along by providing opportunities to casually discuss feelings or situations without judgement. Show them you care and that you're genuinely interested in their happiness.

2. INTPs are not exceptionally well organized, keen on schedules, or great with finances. If you want to build a life with an INTP, you must accept this and accept them. Develop systems, hire help, or take responsibility for the details of your life together.

3. Because they fear being vulnerable or rejected, INTPs can be weary of showing their cards, or putting their heart on the line, too early. They will look for signs that you're not serious or could leave town. If you're serious about them make sure they know it.

4. INTPs spend a lot of their time in their inner world. This world is ripe with creativity and imagination, not to mention the occasional genius. Unfortunately this means the INTP isn't always interested in their outer world and may not be present in thought or emotion with those around them. You must know yourself and know if this is the kind of person you will be happy with.

5. Immature or underdeveloped INTPs don't understand the need for close relationships and would rather spend their time in their heads. In this

case, they may be difficult partners and unwilling to put in the time to make a relationship work.

6.  On the other hand, mature INTPs who have developed a more balanced personality will see the value in their relationships and will be willing to invest their time and emotions into creating a great relationship.

To learn more about how all the types relate and interact, download the free compatibility chart at:

www.DreamsAroundTheWorld.com/thrive

# UNLEASHING YOUR SOCIAL BUTTERFLY AND IMPROVING SOCIAL SKILLS

## SOCIAL SKILLS TRAINING AND ADVICE ON SOCIAL SITUATIONS

In our always-on, always-connected society of e-mail, text messaging and, well, anything but face-to-face conversation, social situations can be a challenge for everyone. We merely do not have as many opportunities to practice conversation as we used to.

As an Introvert, INTPs enjoy time alone and are around others even less than their Extrovert counterparts. This means even less time for the natural practice and development of social skills.

Does this mean Introverts are doomed to a life of awkward interactions and social anxiety? Absolutely not. In fact, it is quite the contrary.

When they invest time into developing their social skills, Introverts can become just as capable in social situations as Extroverts. This gives them a well-rounded personality and an excellent advantage: The ability to chat and socialize when they want, and to sit quietly and listen to others when the situation calls for it. No one likes the person who always has to be the centre of attention right?

This chapter is broken into seven sections, each covering a particular social skill, or kind of social situation. At the end of the chapter you will find a list of additional resources if you would like to continue to work on your social skills.

## BEING INTERESTED

I have heard it said that being interested in others is the fastest route to becoming the most interesting person in the room. Show a genuine interest in others and you will be well liked.

When you take an interest in another person a few powerful things happen.

1 – You build rapport and the other person starts to like you.

2 – You learn important details about the other person. You can then use these details to create conversation around common interests.

When learning about another person, what you ask is almost as important as how you ask it. Typical small talk questions like "So what do you do?" are as boring as they are uninformative. Try using some of the questions below and you will find yourself in much more stimulating conversations.

- What is your biggest goal for this year?
  (Can be followed up by: Why? What challenges do you see coming up?)
- What is your favourite part about your career/hobby/relationship/hometown?
- What is the biggest challenge you are currently facing n your work/school/life?
- I have noticed that you are really good at (insert something you have noticed – for example their style, conversation, telling jokes, business or cooking). What is your secret? Could you share 2 or 3 tips for an amateur like me?

When you are asking questions about their goals or challenges, you are giving yourself an opportunity to offer advice or help them find a solution. You will be amazed at how far this can go, and how much more stimulating the conversation can become when you are working on solving a problem.

In terms of how you approach this, just be curious and thoughtful in your mindset and you will do just fine.

## GETTING OUTSIDE OF YOURSELF

The curious thing is, most people at social events are all thinking the same thing: "I wonder what other people are thinking about me?"

When you come to realize and truly accept this, everything changes. If you are friendly and kind, you will be amazed at how many people will be drawn to you (especially other introverts!).

Of course, much of our anxiety in social situations goes back to the same question playing in our heads: "I wonder what others are thinking about me?"

How do you get past this? Look no further than the last tip: Be genuinely interested in other people. When you move your focus to understanding and caring about others it is almost impossible to focus on yourself at the same time.

## SAY SOMETHING PLEASANT

One compliment can, and will, change someone's whole night.

So why don't we give people more compliments? One reason is that we get stuck in our heads, wondering what to say and how to say it. We worry about coming off as inauthentic, offending someone, or appearing like a kiss ass. We wonder whether our compliment could be misinterpreted, or get us into an awkward situation. Although all these fears are normal, they are also all unfounded.

The key to giving an excellent compliment is in the details, so pay attention to them. Some people spend hours picking out their outfits – nothing is left to chance. Sometimes there will be an obvious "point of pride", such as a new dress or piece of jewelry the person is just waiting to be complimented on. Other times it might not be so obvious, so try these tips:

- For a man, his watch or tie is always a safe compliment (from a man or a woman). From a woman to a man, well, you can get away with complimenting anything.

- For women, jewelry, purses and shoes are always a point of pride and a safe compliment from another woman. For the guys it is a little more complicated. If you don't know the woman well, keep it casual in what you compliment and how you say it. Fashionable jewelry, a trendy phone case or a colourful watch are safe bets and good conversation starters. Follow up your compliment by asking where they got it, or if there is a groovy story behind it. For example, "That's a really cool watch, is there a story behind it?"
  If you already know the woman, a new hairstyle or piece of clothing is also begging for your compliment.

- Always be as authentic as possible. Look for something you do like in someone, whether it is something physical or a character trait. You will never upset someone by mentioning their excellent sense of humor.

- Sometimes you will be able to notice an area someone is trying to improve, and perhaps self-conscious about. For instance, you may notice a fellow introvert making a big effort to be social and tell a story to a group of people. This is an amazing opportunity…use it.

- It's not hard to say "That was really funny, you know, you are a wonderful storyteller". Yet a few kind words on your part here could make an unforgettable impact and go a long way in building their confidence and encouraging them to continue growing. In doing so, not only do you make someone else feel great, you also make them feel good about you.

## PLEASE AND THANK YOU

One of the challenges many introvert types face is a dislike of doing things "just because", particularly when it comes to social norms and etiquette. To the outside world it can appear as rude or inconsiderate when an INTP does not say thank you to their host for having them over for dinner. In reality, the INTP may be very appreciative, they just don't see the need for pleasantries (or they just forgot). They may also take it for granted, assuming the other person knows how much they care about them, or assuming a close friend does not need to be thanked.

The problem is, some people are overly sensitive or just stuck in their ways. Sometimes a lack of "etiquette" can cause unnecessary hostility or conflict, especially with those who do not know you as well, such as a good friend's spouse.

Two things you can do:

**Option 1:** Make an effort to build habits around manners and etiquette. Perhaps it does not make sense to thank someone for passing the salt, but just do it anyway.

**Option 2:** Take a few minutes to speak to, or write a note to, the most important people in your life. Tell them how much you value your relationship and explain to them that social norms are not exactly your thing. Make it clear how much you value them and everything they do for you, even if you do not express it at the moment they do it.

Once a year, say around Christmas, send our handwritten cards to your closest friends and make sure to include a note about how much you appreciate them and how happy you are they are part of your life.

If you do these two things, not only will they not care when you forget a "thank you", you will stand out as one of the most caring and thoughtful people they know.

## EXPLAINING NERVES AND SOCIAL ANXIETY

As we walked into one of our regular cafes, my girlfriend reminded me to say hi to her friend working there. "She was upset you did not say bye last time."

This sparked a conversation on "Hi and Bye" etiquette, and approaching people working or in a group. I explained that most of the time when someone does not come over and say hi they are not trying to be rude. Usually there is something else going on. Often this something else is nervousness, or social anxiety. Approaching a group of people to say hello when you only know one or two of them can cause much stress. Logically it probably should not, but alas, it does. One option is to face the nerves and awkwardly approach the group, standing there waiting to be invited to sit, or for the right time to walk away. The other option is a brief wave, or to pretend you did not see them, and move on. In this case you risk being considered rude, or having people think you do not like them, or are mad at them.

Isn't it funny the wide gap between two people's perceptions?

Unfortunately there is no magic cure for this situation although, for the sake of personal growth, I would encourage you to try to say hello whenever possible.

Although there is no magic cure for the situation, there is a way you can limit the potential damage (and possibly make the situation a lot easier in the future).

The solution is along the same lines as the one in the "Please and Thank You" section. You need to initiate an honest discussion with friends. For an extreme introvert, the idea of being nervous about approaching a group of people is almost confusing. To them, the only possible explanation is rudeness or a disinterest in them.

Yet guess what happens when you explain the situation from your point of view? They start to understand. Not only will they "get it" when you do not approach them within a group, they may even spot you first and come to you to say hello first.

**Note:** In this section I use the term social anxiety to describe nervousness, or anxiety, around situations. If the negative emotions are so strong they negatively influence your life, or the anxiety is constant, we may be talking about a more serious form of social anxiety. If this sounds like you, I encourage you to read: Self Confidence Secrets: How To Overcome Anxiety, Fear and Low Self Esteem With NLP.

I have received many e-mails from readers telling me that book has helped them overcome (sometimes crippling) social anxiety and build their confidence.

## AVOID CRITICIZING AND COMPLAINING

You are at a social event and you feel uncomfortable. You didn't really want to go in the first place, and now you are dreading your decision to "give it a try". You find yourself at the bar when a fellow guest, equally disappointed, strikes up a conversation with you:

"Why are these things always so boring? This might be the worst one yet."

Now it is your turn to speak. How do you respond?

It is easy to fall into this negativity trap. Being critical of others is one of the easiest ways to feel better about yourself (in the moment) and temporarily bond with others. The problem is, it's a short-term solution with many negative long-term consequences. Complaining and criticizing brings you down emotionally, eliminates any drive to become more social, and almost guarantees the night will not get any better.

What is more? When you become a complainer you repel the people you would have the most fun talking with, and the ones who are likely in charge of deciding who will get invited back.

Sure, in that moment, never being invited back may sound like a blessing. Would it not be better to get invited back, and just decline the invitation if you do not want to go?

## ESCAPING THE SMALL TALK TRAP: DIRECT THE CONVERSATION, ASK QUESTIONS, AND GET HELP

Nothing is worse than the *Small Talk Trap*. You are at a social event where you hardly know anyone and find yourself in a conversation with a stranger. Initially the conversation provides relief from the awkward agony of "working the room", but soon the conversation is just as painful. You find yourself thinking back to Biology class wondering how much long-term damage would come from jumping out the second story window behind you and making a run for it.

***It doesn't have to be like this! There is a better way.***

Here are three skills you can use to make your conversations more stimulating.

**Strategy #1 – Direct It.** There is a good chance the other person does not want to talk about the weather any more than you do. Even if they do, why leave it up to them?

When you go to an event, have a few thought-provoking topics in mind. Ideally, these should be interesting to you and the kind of people you like to talk with.. An example could be a book you just read about another culture or a philosophy you have been studying.

When the weather comes up for the 3rd time in a conversation, it is time to change it with this simple phrase:

"Hey, sorry to interrupt but I would love your opinion on something before I forget. I have been reading this book on Stoic philosophy and it has been bombarding me with ideas about how to live life. I keep wondering how these ideas can relate to our modern lifestyle. Do you know much about Stoicism?"

At this point they might be familiar with the topic, excellent. If they are not, it is a chance for you to explain it to them. In doing so, you will crystalize your knowledge of the topic and hopefully teach them something interesting in the process.

Sure, some will not have a lot to say, but others will. Either way, you will have a much better time in this conversation than one about weather or sports!

**Strategy #2 – Ask Questions.** Most people have at least one worthwhile trait or area of knowledge. If you find yourself trapped in a painful conversation, use it as your chance to learn something new.

Start by asking a few quick background questions about the person's home country, work, and hobbies. From there you will be able to find something thought-provoking to zero in on and learn more about. Are they from a far-off country you have always wanted to know more about? Turn this into an opportunity to learn a few phrases in a new language, to discover a few  cultural differences, or ask about possible economic opportunities. Perhaps they study a martial art you have always wanted to learn. You could ask them for advice on the best way to get started, and how to spend your time for the first 3 months.

It won't always be the most fascinating conversation you've ever had, but it's still better than typical small talk.

**Strategy #3 – Get Help.** This one can be trickier, but once mastered, is a ninja skill of social situations. If you are speaking one on one with someone and the conversation is leaving a lot to be desired, try to bring another person in.

The easiest way to do this is when you spot someone you know, or a stranger standing alone, and just motion for them to join you. If this is not an option, there is a plan b. Take the conversation to a point where you need an opinion on something. Perhaps you decide to disagree on what city has the best weather, or which appetizer at the party is best. Whatever it is, use it as an opportunity to seek another opinion from someone walking or standing nearby: "Excuse me, we were just debating this and would love another opinion. What do you think …?"

However you do it, two things can happen when you bring a new person.

One, they could be a stimulating conversationalist and change your night for the better. Often when this happens your original conversation partner will eventually excuse themselves and you will be left with an enjoyable conversation and possibly a new friend. If the conversation does not improve, at least you have given yourself a less awkward escape route because you will not be leaving anyone alone.

Another upside of this approach is that you may be saving someone else from the awkwardness of standing alone and they will be grateful for it.

# ADDITIONAL RESOURCES ON SOCIAL SKILLS

If you enjoyed this section and want to continue your study of people and social skills, here are a few books to get you started.

All the titles below are linked to the book's page on Amazon so you can read more about it.

**Networking for People Who Hate Networking: A Field Guide for Introverts, the Overwhelmed, and the Underconnected**

**Self-Promotion for Introverts: The Quiet Guide to Getting Ahead**

**The Introverted Leader: Building on Your Quiet Strength**

**Quiet: The Power of Introverts in a World That Can't Stop Talking**

**Quiet Influence: The Introvert's Guide to Making a Difference**

**The Introvert Advantage: Making the Most of Your Inner Strengths**

# KEYS TO WEALTH, HEALTH, HAPPINESS AND SUCCESS

I hope this book has provided some insights into how you can succeed in the most important areas of your life.

In this last section, I'd like to share ten strategies to remember that will help you create a balanced and happy life. If you apply them, these strategies will help you enjoy more wealth, health and happiness in your life.

1.   INTPs must follow their strengths and do work that is aligned with their abilities. Take on work that will reward you for your ability to think big and create strategic plans to be successful. Many INTPs find success in very lucrative careers such as investment banking and real estate development.

2.   Face your fears to overcome your weaknesses. Learn to make plans of action and then execute them. This will only happen by taking action and doing it. At first this could be very uncomfortable. Over time you will develop this muscle and it will get easier and easier.

3.   Be accountable and take personal responsibility. It is important to be aware of your weaknesses but do not use this knowledge as an excuse. Never blame others. When you blame others for your circumstances you give away the power to change them. Take responsibility for your life and give yourself the power to change it.

4.   INTPs really dislike repetitive work so stick to "project based" work that allows you to focus on the initial ideas and not worry about execution.

5.  Develop your extroverted intuition – your ability to objectively perceive and understand the outside world. This will help you to form more accurate perceptions of the people and world around you. Spend time really "looking at" the world around you and make an effort to understand it before passing judgement based on your internal thoughts or beliefs.

6.  Value your relationships and the people around you. It may not always feel like it, but these relationships are essential to your happiness, success and sanity.

7.  Plan and schedule time to be around people. When alone for too long, INTPs can get lost in their own thoughts and lose connection with the outside world.

8.  Learn to understand others. You have a unique and wonderful way of looking at the world...but it is one of many and no more right than any others. Learn to understand how other people see the world and your influence will increase while the amount of conflict in your world decreases.

9.  Make time to spend with people and allow your mind to relax...often it is during this "down time" that the best ideas are formulated.

10. It's easy to get trapped in your head or your ideas. Start a hobby or activity that involves something physical, such as a sport, outdoor activity or artistic craft. This will help you get out of your head and connect your ideas with the world around you.

# PRACTICAL SOLUTIONS TO COMMON CHALLENGES

There is an old fashioned attitude that tells us to just tough it up, overcome our weaknesses and do everything.

This is stupid.

If you're an exceptional painter you should spend your time painting and leave the toilet cleaning to someone else. If you struggle with negotiation there is nothing wrong with asking a friend or partner to come along and offer support.

The more you allow yourself to offload the tasks and responsibilities you don't enjoy, the more success you will experience. Here are a few practical ideas for making the most of your strengths while avoiding your weaknesses.

Hire Help With:

- Accounting
- Cleaning
- Laundry
- Planning Travel
- Organization
- Scheduling
- Life Planning (such as a coach)
- Business Planning

# QUOTES FOR THE ENJOYMENT OF INTPS ONLY

To end with I've included a collection of fun, inspiring and relatable quotes for INTPs. Many are from INTPs (real and fictional), others are simply enjoyable for INTPs.

*"Everybody is a genius. But if you judge a fish by its ability to climb a tree, it will live its whole life believing that it is stupid."*

**-ALBERT EINSTEIN**

*"There is something infantile in the presumption that somebody else has a responsibility to give your life meaning and point. The truly adult view, by contrast, is that our life is as meaningful, as full and as wonderful as we choose to make it."*

**-RICHARD DAWKINS**

*"Did you ever stop to think, and forget to start again?"*

### -A. A. MILNE

*"My mind rebels at stagnation. Give me problems, give me work, give me the most abstruse cryptogram, or the most intricate analysis, and I am in my own proper atmosphere. But I abhor the dull routine of existence. I crave for mental exaltation."*

### -ARTHUR CONAN DOYLE

*"People interest me, conversations don't."*

### -GREGORY HOUSE

*"The question isn't who is going to let me; it's who is going to stop me."*

### -AYN RAND

*"I guess I should warn you, if I turn out to be particularly clear, you've probably misunderstood what I said."*

## -ALAN GREENSPAN

*"You must have chaos within you to give birth to a dancing star."*

## -FRIEDRICH NIETZSCHE

*"Nobody realizes that some people expend tremendous energy merely to be normal."*

## -ALBERT CAMUS

*"The individual has always had to struggle to keep from being overwhelmed by the tribe. To be your own man is a hard business. If you try it, you'll be lonely often, and sometimes frightened. But no price is too high to pay for the privilege of owning yourself."*

## -RUDYARD KIPLING

*"I read a book one day and my whole life was changed."*

## -ORHAN PAMUK

*"Weekends don't count unless you spend them doing something completely pointless."*

### -BILL WATTERSON

*"Everything interests me, but nothing holds me."*

### -FERNANDO PESSOA

*"We are currently not planning on conquering the world."*

### -SERGEY BRIN

*"Between two evils, I choose the one I've never tried before."*

### -ROBERT A. HEINLEIN

*"The third-rate mind is only happy when it is thinking with the majority. The second-rate mind is only happy when it is thinking with the minority. The first-rate mind is only happy when it is thinking."*

### -A. A. MILNE

*"I have always imagined that Paradise will be a kind of library."*

**-JORGE LUIS BORGES**


*"My passion is for scientific truth. I don't much care about good and evil. ... I care about what's true."*

**-RICHARD DAWKINS**


*"The cost of sanity in this society, is a certain level of alienation."*

**-TERENCE MCKENNA**

*"The mind is sharper and keener in seclusion and uninterrupted solitude. No big laboratory is needed in which to think. Originality thrives in seclusion free of outside influences beating upon us to cripple the creative mind. Be alone, that is the secret of invention; be alone, that is when ideas are born."*

**-NIKOLA TESLA**

*"When people believe a conclusion is true, they are also very likely to believe arguments that appear to support it, even when these arguments are unsound."*

**-DANIEL KAHNEMAN**

*"There's no point in being nuts if you can't have a little fun."*

**-JOHN NASH**

*"I am an investigator by inclination. I feel a great thirst for knowledge."*

**-IMMANUEL KANT**

*"The naked truth is always better than the best-dressed lie."*

**-ANN LANDERS**

*"Ignorance is not bliss — it is oblivion."*

**-PHILIP WYLIE**

*"The indispensable first step to getting the things you want out of life is this: decide what you want."*

**-BEN STEIN**

*"I just can't — I can't exist in normal group situations. A classroom, where you have to sort of jockey for position, compete for attention — I would just withdraw."*

**-JESSE EISENBERG**


*"He who has a why to live can bear almost any how."*

**-FRIEDRICH NIETZSCHE**


*"I often carry things to read so that I will not have to look at the people."*

**-CHARLES BUKOWSKI**


*"I am free, no matter what rules surround me. If I find them tolerable, I tolerate them; if I find them too obnoxious, I break them. I am free because I know that I alone am morally responsible for everything I do."*

**-ROBERT A. HEINLEIN**

*"The brain is like a muscle. When it is in use we feel very good. Understanding is joyous."*

**-CARL SAGAN**

*"Nothing in life is to be feared, it is only to be understood."*

**-MARIE CURIE**

*"I am free, no matter what rules surround me. If I find them tolerable, I tolerate them; if I find them too obnoxious, I break them. I am free because I know that I alone am morally responsible for everything I do."*

**-ROBERT A. HEINLEIN**

*"If the ability to tell right from wrong should have anything to do with the ability to think, then we must be able to 'demand' its exercise in every sane person no matter how erudite or ignorant."*

**-HANNAH ARENDT**

*"That which can be asserted without evidence, can be dismissed without evidence."*

**-CHRISTOPHER HITCHENS**

*"If you only read the books that everyone else is reading, you can only think what everyone else is thinking."*

**-HARUKI MURAKAMI**


*"The only thing worse than human ignorance is human pride in that ignorance."*

**-GEORGE TAKEI**


*"Sometimes we need silence to let our minds roar."*

**-LAWRENCE BEALL**

# NEXT STEPS

To help you get the most from this book, I have created a collection of free extras to support you along the way. If you haven't already, take a few minutes now to request the free bonuses; you already paid for them when you bought this book. To download these, simply visit the special section of my website: www.dreamsaroundtheworld.com/thrive

There, you will be asked to enter your email address so I can send you the "Thriving Bonus Pack". You'll receive:

1. A 5-part mini-course (delivered via email) with tips on how to adjust your life so you can best make use of your strengths.
2. A compatibility chart showing how you are most likely to relate to the other 15 personality types. You'll discover which types are most compatible with you and which types will likely lead to headaches.
3. A PDF workbook that complements this book. It's formatted to be printed, so you can fill in your answers to the exercises in each chapter as you go.

To download the Thriving Bonus Pack, visit:

www.DreamsAroundTheWorld.com/thrive

# SUGGESTIONS AND FEEDBACK

Like the field of Psychology, this book will always be growing and improving.

If there's something about this book you didn't like, or there is a point you disagreed with, I'd love to hear from you. Perhaps I missed something in my research.

As well, if you're an "experienced" INTP and you'd like to add your personal story, insight, wisdom or advice to upcoming editions, my readers and I would love to hear from you.

To contribute in any way, you can email me at: dan@dreamsaroundtheworld.com.

# Books In The Thrive Personality Type Series

**The ENFP Superhero : Harness your gifts, Inspire others and Thrive as an ENFP**

*Or just visit Amazon and search for "ENFP". Then look for the book by Dan Johnston.*

**INFP Inspired: Embrace your true self and thrive as an INFP**

*Or just visit Amazon and search for "INFP". Then look for the book by Dan Johnston.*

**ENFJ on fire: Utilize your gifts, Change the world and thrive as an ENFJ**

*Or just visit Amazon and search for "ENFJ". Then look for the book by Dan Johnston.*

**INFJ, Heart, Mind and Spirit: A Guide to thriving as an INFJ**

*Or just visit Amazon and search for "INFJ". Then look for the book by Dan Johnston.*

**The Well Rounded ENTJ: Find more harmony, Improve relationships and thrive as a natural leader**

*Or just visit Amazon and search for "ENTJ". Then look for the book by Dan Johnston.*

**INTJ Understood: Harness your strengths and thrive as the unstoppable mastermind**

*Or just visit Amazon and search for "INTJ". Then look for the book by Dan Johnston.*

**The ENTP Plan: Invent yourself, make progress and thrive as the charming and visionary ENTP**

*Or just visit Amazon and search for "ENTP". Then look for the book by Dan Johnston.*

**INTP: Utilize your strengths, solve life's problems and thrive as the genius thinker type INTP**

*Or just visit Amazon and search for "INTP". Then look for the book by Dan Johnston.*

# Thrive Series Collections

**The Idealists: Learning To Thrive As, and With, ENFPs, INFPs, ENFJs and INFJs (A Collection Of Four Books From The Thrive Series)**

**The Rationals: Learning To Thrive As, and With, The INTJ, ENTJ, INTP and ENTP Personality Types (A Collection of Four Books From The Thrive Series)**

# About The Author

Dan Johnston is a #1 international best-selling author, speaker, coach, and recognized expert in the fields of confidence, psychology and personal transformation. As a coach, one of his specialties is helping clients discover their natural talents, apply them to their true purpose and create a plan of action to live the life of their dreams.

Dan publishes new videos weekly on his YouTube Channel. Here you will hundreds of videos on psychology and personality type.

This is the best place to catch Dan's latest content: www.YouTube.com/DreamsAroundTheWorld/

If you prefer to listen, check our Dan's podcast here: www.DreamsAroundTheWorld.com/podcast

**To learn more about Dan Johnston and his coaching services visit:**
www.DreamsAroundTheWorld.com/coaching

For articles, interviews and resources on entrepreneurship, pursuing your passions, travel and creating the life of your dreams, visit Dreams Around The World and subscribe to the "The Life Design Approach":

www.DreamsAroundTheWorld.com


**Find more books By Dan Johnston on his Amazon Author Central Pages:**
Amazon.com:
http://www.amazon.com/author/danjohnston

Amazon.co.uk:
http://www.amazon.co.uk/-/e/B00E1DO6OS

# Exclusive Reader-Only Bonuses:

To help you get the most from this book I have created a collection of free extras to support you along the way.

When you visit the site below you will be able to download a printable workbook to record your reflections and answers to the end of chapter exercises.

You will also receive free enrollment in a Five-Part E-Course on personality psychology delivered by e-mail. The training is packed with tips, strategies, advice and additional resources.

Through the five lessons, you will learn how to implement what you have learnt about your personality type, including:

- How To Learn From Your Mistakes and Gain Experience Fast
- Why You Must, and How You Can, Become The Best In The World
- How to Overcome Your Weak Spots
- How to Put Your Strengths into Action and Achieve Your Highest Potential.
- How To Pay It Forward By Understanding Those Around You and Helping Them Become Their Best Selves

Both are yours free, a special thank you for my readers.

To receive your free companion course and workbook, visit:

**www.dreamsaroundtheworld.com/thrive**

www.ingramcontent.com/pod-product-compliance
Lightning Source LLC
Chambersburg PA
CBHW050041260726
48658CB00005B/1709